# ACKNOWLEDG

MW00900035

I would like to say a huge thank you to everyone who made this book possible. These include but are not limited to: North Shore Gymnastics, Rigert Elite Gymnastics, FlightSchool Gymnastics, all of the coaches who have contributed to my education over the years and all of the gymnasts who participated.

The biggest acknowledgment goes to the wonderful photographer Abigael Kaufman, who was subject to many, many hours in chalk-filled gyms and took each of these beautiful pictures.

*Published: April 16, 2014*
*www.swingbig.org*
*A Swing Big! Publication*

# INTRODUCTION

This is the first full print publication of Swing Big! I wrote this book because when I began coaching, I would scour the internet, attend clinics, stay late to watch practices and do anything I could to get more drills in my head. But I couldn't find a comprehensive resource that was easy to access.

I created this collection of drills because I believe that information should be accessible. I want coaches to be able to pull this book off of the shelf and flip through to find a drill that is useful. The collection is by no means exhaustive, there are hundreds of thousands of drills out there and it is impossible to include them all. That being said, I hope this book provides coaches and gyms with a starting place for how to break down skills.

Use these drills as a jumping off point. Take the ones that work for you and apply them to your program. Get creative—if you find a better way to use a drill, do it. Gymnastics is all about learning and growing (and that includes us as coaches).

I wish you the best with your coaching!

Zari Goldmann
Author and owner of Swing Big!

# 1

# KIPS

These drills are designed to help gymnasts gain the core strength necessary to perform a kip, train the muscle memory for the pull down action and to reinforce correct shapes.

# Hollow holds pushing against bar

This is the very first step I take when teaching kips. If a gymnast cannot stand in a hollow shape and maintain pressure on the bar, there is little chance that she will be able to glide well. This drill can happen very early on in a gymnast's career. I believe that it should be done every day at early compulsory levels

# Glides using octagon or barrel

Performing glides on a barrel or octagon helps the gymnast experience what the extension should feel like at the end of the glide. Also, because the legs are supported, the amount of abdominal strength needed is minimal and the gymnast can gain the muscle memory of keeping her legs straight and focusing on head position.

# Glides kicking blocks or other objects behind feet

Glides are a swing. If there isn't a sufficient jump into the glide and sufficient height in the back swing, the front swing of the glide will lack power. By placing an object behind the gymnast that she has to kick, it ensures that she jumps up in the back and does not immediately pike forward.

# Glides on ball

This is an advanced form of the glides on barrel or octagon drill. This drill can be done with a ball (in this case, the ball has a small bit of sand in it to make it easier), an ab roller or even, in some cases, sliders.

I particularly like this drill because it requires a lot of core stability. In order to keep the ball moving straight back and forth, the gymnast has to be tight and focused on what she is doing.

# Pike holds with toes to bar

This is not so much a drill as a necessary conditioning exercise. While it's true that, with the correct timing, the strength necessary for kips can be drastically cut, a significant amount of abdominal strength is still necessary. This should be a prerequisite for your gymnasts to start kipping.

# Stand still glides, from bent knee hollow body shape

I find a lot of things go wrong in glides as soon as gymnasts jump to the bar. Arms bend, heads go out, shape can be lost, etc. One of my favorite drills for combating this is having gymnasts do their glides from a standstill. Put your gymnast in a hollow position, pushing on the bar with bent knees. Ask her to straighten her knees with a small jump (without letting go of the bar) and perform a glide. The more you do this, the better her shapes will get.

# On the floor, kipping motion to pike compression

This is one of my favorite drills. It's good for strength, it's good for muscle memory, it can be done anywhere, and you can have your kids do it a million times in a day. As soon as your gymnasts can sit up with tight feet and straight knees, it's time to start this drill.

# Stemme kips 2 legs

This is the easier form of stemme kips. You can do it with a block or on the p-bars if you have some. It will feel foreign to your gymnasts at first, but it's critical for them to learn to pull down on the bar with straight arms. I would spot these for a while before letting them go on their own. Once they start bending their arms it's hard to break the habit.

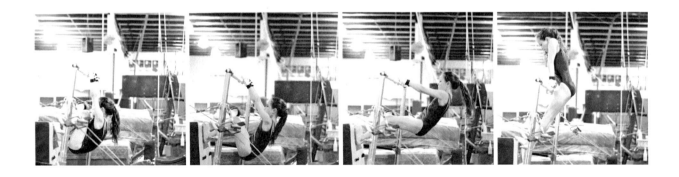

# Stemme kips 1 leg

This is the more advanced form of stemme kips. These require a decent amount of strength and hopefully by the time you are working these your gymnasts are pretty close to their kips.

# Drop kips

Drop kips are just plain necessary. They're not all that fun to spot, but it's hard to ask a gymnast to kip, get down, kip, get down, and kip again in one turn. It just takes too long.

That being said there are ways of making drop kips easier on yourself. Many gyms have a general rule that they will spot drop kips but they won't spot the legs, so the gymnast has to use her own strength to make sure her legs stay on the bar. This also ensures you aren't doing ALL of the work.

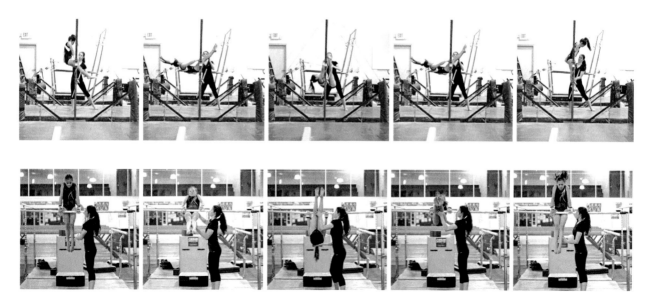

# On floor, lay on back, sit up to compressed pike

This is a drill I like to incorporate into warm ups. It's great conditioning (a lot harder than you would think) and the gymnasts are working kips without even knowing it. The better your gymnasts are at conditioning exercises like these, the better position they will be in to be able to finish their kips and the better they will be able to cast out of them.

# Lat pull downs

This is the main "kipping motion" most of us think of. It's one of those things we want engrained in our gymnasts' muscle memory from the day they walk into the gym so that the kipping process is easier. Many people use their stall bars for leg lifts but I like to use them for lat pulls just as often. They are very similar to two-legged stemme kips except that they are easier because gymnasts aren't actually starting underneath the bar.

# Theraband Pull Downs

This is just another way that gymnasts can work their lats and practice the pulling down action in the kip. I find that it is especially easy to loop a theraband around one of the bases of the bars and have gymnasts do them right after they get off the bar. This is among the easiest side stations to set up.

# Other Exercises:

1. Laying on back on block with hands on bar, lift toes to bar and lower

2. L holds hanging from bar.

3. Tuck holds hanging from bar (hollow shape).

4. Laying on back in pike position, pull theraband from overhead to hips.

5. Hollow holds with back on physio ball with coach assistance.

6. Hollow holds and rocks.

7. Jump from spring board in hollow shape, push on bar with straight arms, land back on floor.

8. Pike forward rolls to stand.

# 2

# CAST HANDSTANDS

These drills are to teach gymnasts how to get their hips above their head, eliminate the fear of being upside down, reinforce correct shapes, develop shoulder strength, and teach gymnasts how to push down on the bar.

# Pike ups on ball

This is the perfect drill to use for beginning gymnasts to start figuring out how to get their hips over their heads. Because of the piked position, it's hard for them to arch their backs, which is a common problem. It also requires a decent amount of core strength. This is one of my first drills for gymnasts learning to cast handstand because it teaches good muscle memory from the beginning.

# Shoulder extensions both on hands and elbows

This drill helps teach gymnasts how their shoulder action affects their casts. The shoulder blades need to come together as their legs swing forward in the cast and then separate and push down on the bar as the cast occurs.

# One leg pike handstand

Just being able to get to handstand is not enough. Once your gymnast gets there, it is imperative that she is in the correct shape. It can be hard to correct shapes in a full handstand, but correcting gymnasts' shapes in a pike handstand or one leg pike handstand is much easier. This type of handstand helps them understand what ribs-in means and how their back and head should feel in a handstand.

# Press from panel mat

Presses have earned their reputation as good cast handstand drills/conditioning exercise because they very well mimic the motion that gymnasts will do on the bar. However, some gymnasts are just not strong enough yet to perform a press from the ground correctly. For these gymnasts, it would be a good use of time to have them press off of a panel mat if you have too many to spot or are busy doing something else.

# Press-ups between panel mats

Like with the previous drill, gymnasts who are not yet capable of performing a full press to hand-stand can still get many of the benefits from performing this drill. This drill helps develop the same muscles and teaches them to lean their shoulders over their hands without the same amount of strength required.

# Spotted cast handstands

Spotted cast handstands are absolutely necessary. Without them, some gymnasts will never get over their fear of being in/getting to handstand. They are also a good way to correct shapes and for you to actually FEEL what your gymnasts are doing wrong. If you can feel their shoulders pushing back against you, i.e. not leaning over the bar, you then have a better idea of how to help them.

# From straddle stand on floor bar, jump to handstand

This drill is one of my absolute favorites because there is no way to do it without leaning your shoulders over the bar. This is the biggest point of fear with most gymnasts; so, training it on the floor for months before putting it on the bar is the best idea.

# Pike ups with sliders

This drill is very similar to the pike up with the ball drill. For gyms that do not have physio balls on hand, or don't have enough of them, this is a good alternative. A slider, paper plate or Frisbee will do just fine.

# Handstand lever drill

This drill helps gymnasts understand the levering action that happens with cast handstands, builds strength, and provides a good environment (i.e. on the ground) to fix shapes before putting it on the bar. I think it also helps gymnasts learn that leaning over the bar is required in a way where it doesn't feel like they are about to fall to their death.

# Stalder hold drill

This drill is excellent for any of your gymnasts but especially those who have problems arching their backs and sticking their heads out in casts. This drill teaches the gymnast how to push down on the bar in the correct body position.

# Pike ups on bar

This is one of my favorite drills. This is actually a drill you can start very, very early. I even do it with more advanced recreational gymnasts. My favorite way to do it is on a LOW, LOW bar with a couple soft mats on the other side of the bar. Gymnasts push up as far as they can and then forward roll over. It helps with the fear of falling forward. Note: I spend a decent amount of time spotting these at first. I always start doing this drill in regular grip. You can start doing it on a spotting block first as it helps gymnasts build confidence and strength before moving to a real bar. This drill both gets gymnasts leaning of the bar AND pushing down on it. Once they are proficient doing this in a normal grip, I start having them do it in reverse grip. Getting your gymnasts on the bar and comfortable in all different grips is incredibly important. This is an easy way to build strength and get them comfortable in reverse grip at the same time.

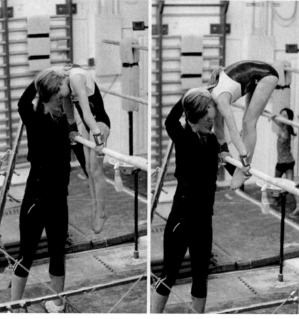

# Knees to handstand

I've found that, for gymnasts, starting from their knees more accurately recreates the feeling of starting from a front support. Even though they aren't casting, it does seem to give them a better appreciation of how far they have to go to get their hips over their hands.

# Stalder sliders

This is an excellent drill for a beginning cast handstand progression. The gymnast is gaining a large amount of the core strength necessary to lift her hips up and get her feet in to her hands, and is also drilling the same muscle memory that will be necessary on the bar when she casts.

# Straddle and pike to handstand

This drill is a good simulation of last part of the cast to handstand, and helps the gymnast build the necessary muscles. The other thing I like about the drill is that, when teaching straddle cast handstands, many gymnasts get stuck in that bent arm, head stuck out body position, and this drill will help prevent that. The more of these your gymnasts do in a correct body position, the better luck you are going to have preventing that shape from happening.

# Shoulder rocks on floor bar

The goal of this drill is very similar to that of pike ups on the bar. One of the biggest problems that occurs when gymnasts learn to cast handstand is that their shoulders start going the wrong direction. A lot of this comes from fear, which can be combated with the pike up drill, but it also comes from a lack of awareness of where their shoulders are. This drill aids both shoulder and core strength (especially if you are using a physio ball) and it also helps gymnasts to become aware of where "shoulders over the bar" actually is.

# Press walks forward

I like this drill for developing shoulder strength and body position. The last part of a straddle cast handstand (bringing the legs together) is often the easiest. Getting the gymnast to the point where she is confident and strong with her shoulders over the bar in a stalder position is often the most difficult. This exercise helps with that.

# Other Exercises:

1. Cast holds with feet elevated and pointed

2. Start holding weight with both hands (sitting or standing) then lift above head with straight arms (maintaining good back shape)

3. Casts in a row - progressively higher

4. Casts with theraband connecting standards, heels against theraband

# 3

# PIROUETTING

These drills are designed to develop awareness of handstand position, to develop proper technique of shoulder extension and openness, to create the ability to shift weight and to develop correct shapes throughout pirouette.

# Straight arm hand flips in push-up

This is the first pirouetting drill that I teach gymnasts. In order to get a nice strong pirouette, gymnasts need to be able to transfer their weight from arm to arm with straight arms, without collapsing, and without compromising their body shape. As soon as your gymnasts can hold a good push-up shape with straight arms you can begin doing this drill.

# Straight arm hand flips in front support

Another variation of this drill is to do it in front support. I like doing this type of work at all angles, from front support up to handstand, just because it raises the gymnast's comfort level dramatically.

As the gymnast gets more comfortable, she is better able to focus on body shapes and technique.

# Straight arm hand flips in pike handstand

Pike handstands are one of my favorite drills. I think they are especially important for pirouettes. They allow gymnasts to feel what it will be like to pirouette with their hips over their head but without their ribs or head sticking out in a way that prevents them from pirouetting on top of the bar. By combining a pike handstand with the straight arm hand flip, you give the gymnast a more accurate feeling of pirouetting in a good shape.

# One armed handstand hand lifts (small)

This is just another variation of the weight shifting drills. Before gymnasts go on to the next drill (one arm handstands), you should make sure they have done this drill to proficiency.

# Straight arm hand flips in pike handstand

One arm handstand holds are essential for pirouettes, as weight transfer is essential, and gymnasts need to be comfortable being on one arm for more than a millisecond. Unless your gymnasts are comfortable on one arm, they will never be truly comfortable pirouetting and therefore their pirouettes will be hurried, not on top of the bar, and their focus will not be on their shapes. Make sure the feet are slightly tilted when gymnasts are on one arm.

# Pirouettes hanging from high bar

This is a drill I love doing with young gymnasts for teaching blind changes. Explaining which direction and how to turn can often be difficult, but this drill makes it easy for them to remember. It builds muscle memory really early, so that, when they turn upside down to do it for real, it is exponentially easier for them.

# Mill circle walks

The more comfortable your gymnasts are shifting their weight from one arm to the other, the better their pirouettes will be. But even more importantly, good pirouettes require a decent amount of shoulder strength. This is a great way to introduce weight shifting and build strength after you've done the progressions in a push-up position and in front support.

# Mill circle walks reversed

This drill uses the same rationale as the one before but has the added benefit of getting your gymnast comfortable with being in reverse grip.

# Handstand pirouette fall to back

A lot of gyms do this drill where the gymnast kicks up to handstand, does a handstand pirouette and falls to her stomach or push-up position. The problem is that this encourages a late pirouette. The version of the drill shown below is different in that having her fall to her back encourages an early pirouette and helps the gymnast learn how to turn with her shoulders and hips on top of her hands.

# Handstand ½ pirouette against wall

In this drill, the gymnast pirouettes and her feet maintain contact with the wall the entire time. It may almost feel to your gymnast like she is pirouetting on the wrong side of the bar. You should encourage her that this is the feeling she should be trying to achieve when she pirouettes out of a cast handstand.

# Handstand ½ pirouette with ¼ turn hold in the middle

This pirouetting drill starts with the gymnast's stomach on the wall. She then flips her first hand, performs a quarter pirouette (with feet still on the wall) and then the second 1/4 pirouette.

The 1/4 pirouetting technique ensures that the gymnast is pushing tall throughout the entire pirouette. Also, because the feet are always in contact with the wall, it ensures that the entire pirouette is done in handstand. Ask your gymnast if this feels a little strange. She will generally say yes, but it is correct. You should instruct her to try and recreate that feeling when she is on the bar.

# ½ pirouette from reverse grip against wall

This drill has the same rationale as the previous drills but is starting from a reverse grip.

# Back extension roll to one arm

When pirouetting out of a giant (or any circle), gymnasts need to understand that the pirouette has to begin before they get to handstand. Otherwise, they will finish late. This drill is something you can do on the floor to start preparing your gymnast to pirouette early. Note: this should be spotted at first and it can get ugly (read: they may end up on their head if their arms bend), so be aware the first few times you have your kids try it.

# Pirouettes inside a box

This drill can be done with tape on the floor or chalk on the floor. The goal is to get gymnasts to pirouette with their shoulders over their hands. In order to stay inside the box the gymnast has to maintain a relatively straight line.

# Other Exercises:

1. Standing on feet with holding weighted bar above head. Flip first hand and turn bar as if performing pirouetting action.

2. Kip, cast handstand 1/4 turn. Flip first hand and perform 1/4 turn (keeping one hand off the bar).

3. From knees on floor with hands on floor bar -- perform straddle up handstand with 1/2 pirouette ending with stomach against wall.

4. Shoulder shrugs in handstand and pike handstand

5. Small cast with hand flip

6. Hollow rocks roll turn to plank (push-up position on elbows) -- turning with toes first.

7 Handstands walks (short steps) across the floor bar with stomach against wall.

# 4

# CLEAR HIPS

These drills are designed to train the drop back for the clear hip, create good shapes and to develop muscle memory for the opening portion of the clear hip.

# Spotted clear hip drops

One of the most important parts of the clear hip is teaching gymnasts how to lean their shoulders back quickly and efficiently. This can be scary for some gymnasts, especially if they let their heads come out. Start with small casts (or bigger casts that you slow down) and help your gymnasts feel safe enough to lean back quickly and aggressively.

# Thera-band extension

This drill is for the opening part of the clear hip. It helps the gymnast develop both the muscle and muscle memory to open from a compressed position to what will eventually turn into handstand. Unless these muscles are developed properly, that will never happen. This is a good drill for teaching gymnasts how to do that without letting their ribs pop out and their arms bend.

# Feet on ball overhead opens

This drill has a similar purpose to the last one but requires substantially more core strength. In these pictures, the gymnast is holding sticks to simulate holding the bar but, as the gymnast becomes better at this drill, I prefer to add a weight.

# Small clearhips from hollow shape (no cast)

This is one of the big places shaping comes in for me. Because the gymnast does not cast, I have sufficient time (and a sufficiently slow gymnast) that I can fix her shape fairly easily. This is also a good drill for fixing any arm bend you may see and generally building confidence by doing a smaller, slower version of the eventual skill.

# Double back hip circles

Double back hip circles provide a good drill to teach the necessary wrist shift for clear hips. If your gymnast cannot perform a double back hip circle with straight arms, chances are that she is not going to have the necessary wrist shift to perform a clear hip. Due to this, the clear hip will most likely have bent arms and result in poor shapes.

# Back extension rolls

Back extension rolls are the staple drill for clear hips. That is because they so well replicate the opening action that occurs in the skill. When gymnasts are proficient at back extension rolls to handstand you can have them "hop" near the top of the handstand and switch their hands so they are facing forward. This can replicate the timing of the wrist shift and also some of the feeling of it. If gymnasts cannot perform these with good shapes, you can always do them off of panel mats to make them a little easier.

# Other Exercises

1. From candle stick (elevated), hollow over floor or tramp bar to push-up position.

2. Start from push-up position with hands on floor bar and feet on ball (or octagon), extend (push backward) to "handstand" (extended position) with hands on floor bar and feet on ball.

3. Back extension rolls with Forster bar or octagonal floor bar.

4. Drop from handstand to horizontal (hands on floor bar) ending with feet on resi-mat.

5. Clear hips from and to a block (eliminate the cast).

6. Shaping rocks in lowered kip wheel. Sit in kip wheel, hold hollow position pushing on bar. Rock from shoulders over the bar to shoulders beneath the bar multiple times.

7. Clear hips with foam under chin to keep head in.

# 5

# RECREATIONAL CLASSES

This chapter will give you ideas for drills that you can do with your recreational classes on bars. You can use drills from other chapters as well, but finding enough things to do with recreational classes on bars can be challenging. This chapter is meant to give you a few more options.

# Arch hold

Body shape identification is one of the most important things we teach young gymnasts. Before we ask them to perform skills in which they have to move from one shape to another, we need them to be able to hold the shapes individually and well. I specifically like to have gymnasts do this drill with the foam because it keeps their arms close to their ears.

# Back hip circle falls

One of the hardest parts about back hip circles is getting gymnasts to lean their shoulders back, especially without piking. In order to reinforce this feeling early you can do back hip circle falls on a resi mat or, really, any super soft mat. My favorite way to do it is having the gymnast hold onto something resembling a bar (ex: PVC pipe or dowel) because that makes it even more similar to what she will feel on the bar.

# Chin ups with feet on block

Chin ups are necessary as gymnasts join the competitive ranks, but the strength required is often far above what recreational gymnasts are able to do. In order to help gymnasts be successful in learning things like pull overs, we need to give them strength exercises that are easier to do. This version of chin-ups is perfect for recreational classes as it is still a very good strength builder but allows recreational gymnasts to be successful early on.

# Floor bar mill circle drill

Shoot throughs for mill circles are not something I like to do with lower level recreational gymnasts. They require a decent amount of strength to get a good cast and often gymnasts are afraid of falling forward, and this can create bad habits of not leaning forward so as to not fall. Instead, I prefer to use drills like this one to simulate the motion in a safe environment until I feel that they have the requisite strength. This drill can be done with a set up like this or even on a medium beam if one is available.

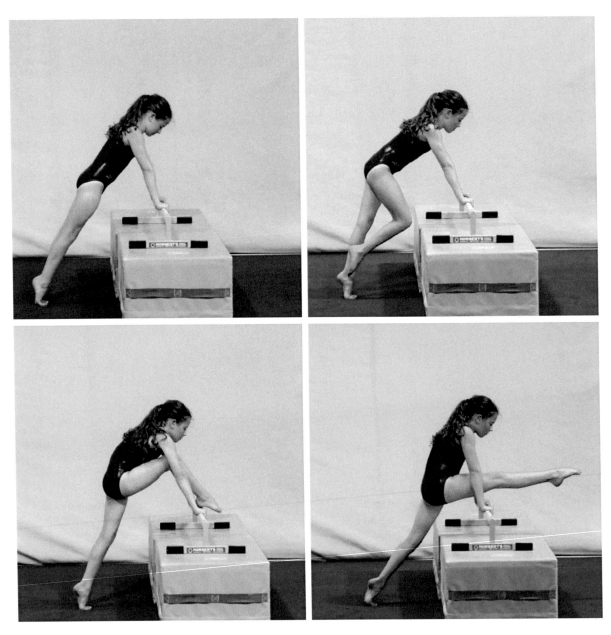

# Push up hold on floor bar

I hear so many coaches teaching casts say "belly in, belly in." While this is a legitimate correction, if the gymnast has never been put in a cast position before it may be unrealistic to expect them to know what that means. That's why one of my favorite side stations, going as far back as very beginning recreational classes, is push-up holds on a floor bar (my preference is feet pointed). This reinforces, very early, that this is the shape we use for casting. Start with a block and move to a physio ball as gymnasts get stronger.

# Teeter totters on floor

Teaching gymnasts to hold a straight body is necessary. But, as they progress in their gymnastics, we have to find a way to teach them to maintain that shape while moving, swinging, circling etc. These teeter totters are a very introductory way to introduce the concept of maintaining shape. I like to have them hold a dowel or PVC pipe to mimic what they will feel in a back hip circle.

47

# Walking pull-overs

It's hard to spot a lot of pull overs in a recreational class. It often limits you to one place so you can't help other gymnasts and it can be taxing on the spotter's body. In order to combat this fatigue/strain, you can have a walking pull-over station. It allows gymnasts to be self-sufficient when doing pull overs which in turn also boosts their confidence, and allows you to move around the class helping others who may need you.

# Feet up on block flat body hold

While teaching gymnasts to have a straight body is important, teaching them to have a straight body and be tight at different angles is essential. This drill builds abdominal strength, and also helps gymnasts identify where straight is, which is especially good for things like back hip circles. If you have PVC pipe or a large dowel you can also have the gymnasts hold that, which can make it an even better simulation.

# Other Exercises

1. Hanging from high bar, hand walks across

2. Tuck inverted hang

3. Front support between p-bars, and mimic shoot through motion

4. Holding squat position on floor bar

5. Swings in straddle hang with feet on bar

— 6 —

# MISCELLANEOUS DRILLS

This chapter is a combination of all of the drills and conditioning exercises that didn't particularly have a place in the other chapters.

# Arch rocks

Even as we teach gymnasts how to hold shapes like arch, hollow and straight body, we have to teach them how to maintain those shapes while in motion. So once gymnasts have a proficient arch hold and tight body, you can start having them do arch rocks. When they do these, I always want their ears covered (partially why I often have them hold a block) and make sure their shoulders are fully extended, meaning their shoulders are all the way in their ears.

  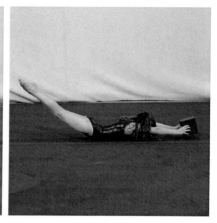

# Extensions on barrel

Extensions develop core strength and shapes, but more than anything this is a great drill for shaping tap swings and giants. More often than not, I find that gymnasts don't understand what pushing on the bar feels like. With this drill, I can help them find the shape I want in the skill and also ensure their shoulders are extended and pushing continuously. (If they aren't, more often than not they will collapse).

# Tuck hold

This is a great drill for both shaping and shoulder strength. As you can see, the gymnast's shoulders are over her hands, reinforcing that position and her back is rounded. You can also help the gymnast turn upside-down into a tuck handstand which helps her learn how to maintain that nice round shape in her back.

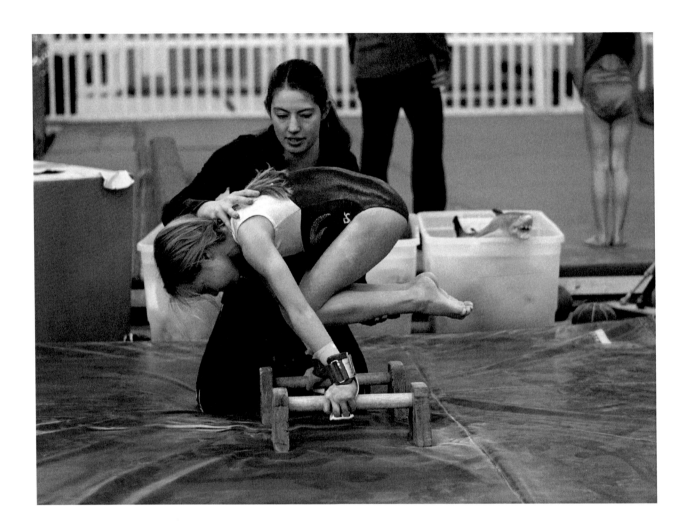

# Pike hold

This is a nice side conditioning exercise if you've got a spare pair of parelletes lying around or are near a beam. If abdominal and shoulder strength are something that you want to work, this is an easy drill to add.

# Pike throughs

This is a great drill for a whole bunch of reasons. The initial part from push up to pike is good for abdominal strength, especially the kind needed in kips and cast handstands. The middle mimics the compression needed for toe circles and in bar circles and the extension at the end mimics the part of many skills that goes from compression to open. Note that coming back the opposite direction is much harder.

# Stalder extension to candle stick

There are so many things that you can do to drill stalders before gymnasts are actually ready to start putting them on the bar (and even when they are). I particularly like this drill because it helps drill the muscle memory for the second half of the stalder. Going from compression to a flat hips candle stick shape will help the gymnast understand the second half of the stalder without having to perform it.

# Stalder extension roll

This drill simulates a stalder in the floor as well any other drill I've found. It's a similar idea to how we use back extension rolls for clear hips, except I find this drill slightly more effective, because the drop from handstand to push-up helps simulate the drop into the stalder. The one thing you want to make sure of is that the gymnast's shoulders don't go in front of her hands.

# Tap swing drill low bar

I like this drill because there is no high bar involved. This is a station gymnasts can do on their own as a side station over and over again in order to build muscle memory. I also like that it keeps their feet behind them a decent ways because I think it gives a more accurate feeling than the following tap swing drill on high bar, although both have their benefits.

# Tap swing drill high bar

The transition between hollow and arch in tap swings can be one of the most confusing parts of tap swings for young gymnasts. Often it just does not feel natural. By doing shape transitions hanging from the high bar, gymnasts build a lot of muscle memory so that, when you finally ask them to tap swing, the transition between shapes is smoother.

# Windshield wipers

Normal leg lifts work the abdominals and hip flexers, but in order to get the obliques and other muscles involved, some variation is required. In order for gymnasts to have good "core" strength, all of their core muscles need to be strong, not just a few. If you are tired of just having your gymnasts do leg lifts or feel that your core strength may be lacking, this exercise will help.

# Handstands At Angles

This is one exercise that I like to do to reinforce the round back that I like to see in various skills on bars.

# Levers on Springboard

This is a great abdominal exercise. You can do it on a springboard like this or with your gymnast holding the lowest rung of a set of stall bars. As you can see in these pictures. I'm spotting, which I generally do until I'm sure the gymnast can do the exercise without a hip angle on the way up.

# Reverse Grip Handstand Holds

Our gymnasts spend an enormous amount of time in a regular grip on bars, but, in order for gymnasts to be successful in reverse grip and other grips, they need to be used to them, too. One way to do this is to have gymnasts perform handstand holds (or pike handstand holds) in alternate grips. That way, when those skills come about, there is one less thing to get used to.

# Flyaway Drill

This is a nice introductory flipping drill for flyaways. The gymnast starts laying flat (close to approximately the position she will let go of the bar in), and then lets the rotation just happen from the spotter. It's a nice way to get gymnasts used to flipping and to increase air awareness.

# Other Exercises and Conditioning

1. Cast holds with feet on block and hands on physio ball

2. Dips on p-bars

3. Ab rollers

4. Planch hold, toes pointed, feet elevated, place hand on hip and twist to the side

5. L to L leg lifts

6. Leg lifts with foam block between knees (knees bent at 90 degrees), curl up to tuck position maintaining 90 degree knee bend

# CONCLUSION

---

This marks the end of this book. I hope that the information and drills have been helpful. These exercises are meant to give you a base platform for your bars coaching and to provide building blocks you can work with within your program. I believe that if you start using these drills planfully and consistently you will see a dramatic increase in your gymnasts' skills on bars.

So go forth, work hard, and remember excellence takes time. Don't give up, don't forget the details, and be sure to have fun along the way!

Zari Goldmann
Author and Owner of Swing Big!

Made in the USA
Middletown, DE
23 February 2016